BOLD KIDS

Michigan

CHILDREN'S PEOPLE AND PLACES BOOK

For the youngest of kids, here are some facts about Michigan: First, the state is the 26th most populous in the union. Its motto is "Si quaeris peninsulam amoenam, look around."

Known for its lakes and many national parks, Michigan is a gorgeous place to visit. Its name comes from two Latin words meaning "if you seek a pleasant peninsula, look around."

The Mackinac Bridge is five miles long and took three years to build. In 1939, Henry Ford invented the assembly line and created the first air-conditioned car in Michigan.

In 1622, two French explorers made the first known sighting of Lake Superior. Native Americans in the area include the Ottawa, Ojibwa and Pottawatomi. The state is also home to the largest suspension bridge in the world, the Mackinac.

The Mackinac Bridge is five miles long and took three years to build. Despite the huge population, the bridge is still in use today. The first phone system in the world was developed in 1879 and has been in operation for 125 years. Another fascinating fact about Michigan is that it was home to the inventor of the assembly line, Henry Ford.

In 1939, the auto giant created the first air-conditioned car in the world. The state has the longest freshwater shoreline in the world, more than twice as much as Alaska, with more than 11,000 inland lakes. In addition, Michigan is home to more than 36,000 miles of streams and 116 lighthouses.

There are some interesting things about Michigan that your kids will enjoy learning about. In addition to its beautiful landscape, this state is home to a number of famous people and is a popular fishing destination.

Founders Brewing Company in Grand Rapids has been named the second-best brewery in the world in 2012 and is a great place for family vacations. Among the most famous attractions, the Henry Ford Museum is located in Detroit. This museum displays items from Thomas Edison's laboratory and Rosa Parks' bus.

Other interesting facts about Michigan are the state's history. For instance, it was the first city to use telephone numbers. In 1939, Henry Ford invented the assembly line, which is the basis for the modern automobile.

In 1622, two French explorers visited Michigan and saw Lake Superior. The original inhabitants of the state were the Ottawa, Ojibwa, and Pottawatomi Indians.

Aside from its scenic landscape, Michigan is home to several interesting animals. For example, the state has five peninsulas and has no wolverines.

The city is also home to five-lined skinks and red bellied snakes, as well as spiny soft-shell turtles. Throughout history, people have lived and worked in Michigan. So, you should learn the names of these animals and learn more about their habitat.

The nickname "Wolverine State" is an apt one for this state. It originated from a dispute over the strip of land between the two states. The term "Wolverine" is also used to describe people of the state.

It has a history of bloodshed. This is why the state is so unique. So, why not learn more? Try these interesting facts about Michigan for kids!

Aside from the many fascinating facts about wildlife, Michigan is also home to the longest suspension bridge in the world. Its nickname was born from a dispute over Toledo. As a result, the state was known as "bloodthirsty."

The naming was also derived from a conflict over the strip between the two states. These interesting facts about Michigan will make your child's mind wonder. And he or she will appreciate the soaring and majestic Mackinac Bridge.

Michigan is home to the world's longest suspension bridge, the Mackinac. Its population is estimated at 5.3 million. The state borders four Great Lakes. Its population is divided between the Upper and Lower peninsulas. For children, this state has some unusual and interesting facts.

Moreover, there are many fascinating places to visit in Michigan, including Detroit and the Upper Peninsula. If you're looking for interesting facts about Michigan, this information will surely help you decide where to go next.

9 781071 710630